ZERO TRUST

PROACTIVE CYBER SECURITY FOR EVERYONE

TROY WILLIAMS MSITM, PI

Printed in the United States of America
First Printing 2022
First Edition 2022

10 9 8 7 6 5 4 3 2 1

ZERO TRUST

Table of Contents

Foreword

How My Journey Started

In 1990 I worked as a store manager at Radio Shack in Lebanon, Tennessee. Many customers came to the store each week wanting to know how to record a phone call, and I sold them a Phone recorder, 120min HD tapes, Batteries, and a recording module. I did not ask any questions, but I knew what they were doing: they were trying to catch their cheating spouse.

So, this gave me the idea that there must be more to this than just recording cheating spouses, and that's when I decided to see how to become a Private Investigator (PI).

That same year I attended my wife's high school reunion and told her classmates that I was tired of retail and mentioned that I wanted to become a PI. They challenged me to quit Radio Shack on a coin toss. Heads, I leave…Tails I don't….and it was fate that I lost (actually 'won') that bet.

The rest is history. I started Information Systems Detective Agency in Jan of 1993 and left Radio Shack.

Through the years, I worked on many domestic and criminal cases and even, at one point, was a bail enforcement agent (Bounty Hunter) in Nashville, Tn. I was young and eager to try every type of Criminal and Civil investigation. I never turned down any case. I was determined to make a name for myself and be the person that would solve any issue.

I was like a sponge; I took every type of online class and went to every industry seminar to learn as much information about this industry as possible. My current training is still with the same company, SBI seminars in Dothan, Alabama, and owner John Gormley. John has become a very close friend, and we discuss law and cases to keep me up to date on the industry.

I made a career change into Cyber Security as things in the investigation industry have changed drastically since 1990, and I wanted to be a part of that. In 2020 I went back to school at Western Governors University Tennessee and obtained my bachelor's in Cyber Security and Information Assurance and then again in 2022, Master's in information technology management. I can help consumers and businesses with Pro-Active Cyber-attacks and online security with this advanced knowledge.

I need to thank my wife, Angela, for listening to all my crazy investigation stories over the years and believing that I could go back to school at this age in my life. I also thank all my mentors and instructors at Western Governors University; they were instrumental in getting me through some tough exams. When I started college, I put together a vision board, and on that board, I added all my past and future goals. I have met all of them. I could have never made it without that vision board and the people surrounding me. We all need a support system, and God has blessed me with that.

Introduction

In the wake of high-profile data breaches, cyber-attacks are more rampant than ever. You must employ proactive cyber security measures to keep your business and data safe. One such measure is Zero Trust. In these recent times, cyberattacks are becoming increasingly common; it's vital to have a security strategy that doesn't rely on perimeter defenses. Cybersecurity is not only a technical challenge but also a policy problem. The current "Castle and Moat" security paradigm is no longer effective in today's interconnected world. A new, more proactive approach is needed to protect our digital assets and prevent cyber threats. The cybersecurity landscape is constantly evolving, with new threats always emerging. Policymakers must be constantly aware of these threats and how they can impact individuals, businesses, and governments. Everyone needs to understand the basics of cybersecurity to be able to protect themselves and their data.

In the old days, keeping the bad guys out was easy. IT departments would establish a perimeter of firewalls and intrusion detection systems and feel reasonably safe with their data inside the enterprise. But with the advent of mobile devices, cloud computing, and social media, that perimeter has disappeared. This has brought a concept that is now more important than ever – proactive cyber security. Zero trust is a proactive approach to cybersecurity that helps organizations protect their data and systems from cyberattacks. This helps to prevent unauthorized users from gaining access to confidential data, which could lead to a data breach.

Zero Trust is a security model that assumes that users inside the network are just as likely to be malicious as those outside the network. With the proper security measures in place, enterprises can protect themselves against attacks. It is a necessary step in today's increasing cyber threats and is essential for organizations that want to protect their data and systems from cyberattacks. By verifying everyone who tries to access an internal resource, IT departments can ensure that only authorized users can access sensitive information. This can be a daunting task for businesses with large user populations, but it's necessary for keeping your data safe.

This proactive cyber security approach is necessary because the enterprise's perimeter has become much less defined in today's world. With people working primarily from offices using on-premises data centers, IT departments could feel reasonably safe with perimeter defenses against cyberattacks. However, with more and more people working remotely and using cloud-based resources, the perimeter has become much more porous. IT departments can no longer rely on perimeter defenses to protect their systems from cyberattacks.

I believe that proactive cyber security is essential for everyone. By securing our networks and data, we can reduce the risk of cyber-attacks and protect our valuable information. Now, enterprises must adopt a zero-trust security model, meaning they must not trust anyone or anything and verify them whenever they try to access an internal or external resource. Enterprise systems must be secure not just from the outside world but from insiders. Every employee, contractor, and partner must be considered a potential threat, and their access to data and systems must be monitored and restricted as necessary.

However, the key to successfully implementing the Zero Trust security model is comprehensive visibility into all users, devices, and traffic. This visibility can be achieved through network activity monitoring, user activity monitoring, and device activity monitoring.

Zero Trust security is based on the following principles:

1. Never trust, always verify: All users and devices must be verified before granting access to any resources.
2. Least privilege: Users and devices should only be given the minimum access necessary to perform their tasks.
3. Defense in depth: Multiple layers of security should be used to protect resources.
4. Continuous monitoring: Security posture should be continuously monitored and updated in response to environmental changes.

Zero Trust Pro-Active Cyber Security is a security model that assumes that users can gain access to resources from any device, location, and network. The security model prevents attackers from accessing sensitive data or systems. Zero Trust Pro-Active Cyber Security uses various security measures to protect data, including firewalls, intrusion detection systems, and antivirus software.

Reactive cyber security is a defensive strategy that relies on identifying and responding to cyber-attacks after they have occurred. Proactive cyber security is a preventive strategy that identifies and mitigates potential cyber threats before they can cause harm.

There is no one-size-fits-all answer to this question, as the cost of implementing proactive cyber security will vary depending on the specific security measures used. However, pro-active cyber security is often seen as a more cost-effective option than reactive cyber security, as it can help to prevent cyber-attacks from happening in the first place.

When it comes to cyber security, one of the biggest threats that people face is identity theft. Identity theft can occur when someone steals your personal information and uses it to commit fraud or other crimes. There are many different methods that scammers use to steal your personal information, and below are some of the most common ones:

Proactive Measures to Stop Scams

- Educating users about cyber security and how to spot scams

- Implementing cyber solid security policies and procedures

- Using firewalls and intrusion detection systems

- Training employees in cyber security best practices

- Regularly backing up data

Another vital step to protecting yourself from cybercriminals is to use strong passwords and change them regularly. You can create strong passwords by combining letters, numbers, and symbols and avoiding common words or phrases. You should also never use the same password for more than one account.

Cybercriminals are constantly on the lookout for anything of value. This can include personal information, financial data, or even just access to your computer or device. They use this information to commit identity theft, fraud, or other crimes.

cybercriminals are also known for launching cyber-attacks, which can disable entire systems and networks.

The best way to protect yourself from cyber criminals is to be vigilant about safeguarding your personal information. This includes not giving out your passwords or PINs and being careful about what you share online. You should also install anti-virus software on your computer and keep it up to date. Additionally, make sure you have a strong password that is difficult to guess.

Common Scams:

The One Ring Phone Scam:

It is a scam that uses a fake caller ID to trick victims into answering calls from numbers they do not recognize. The scammer poses as a representative from a legitimate organization, such as a bank or utility company, and asks for personal information or money.

To protect yourself from the One Ring' Phone Scam, never give your personal information or money to someone you don't know. If you receive a call from a number you don't recognize, don't answer it. And if you do answer it and the caller asks for personal information or money, hang up immediately.

Amazon Prime Scam:

Amazon Prime Day is a great time to snag some fantastic deals on items you've been wanting. But as you start your shopping preparations, it's important to be aware of the various scams that cybercriminals will try to use to steal your money and personal information.

One common scam is fake emails or texts that claim to be from Amazon, notifying you of a great deal on a product. The email might include a link to a website where you can supposedly buy the product. However, this website is a scam designed to steal your personal information.

Another common scam around Prime Day is phishing websites. Phishing websites are websites that look legitimate but are created by scammers to steal your personal information. So, be careful about which websites you visit and make sure that the web address starts with "HTTPS" rather than just "HTTP".

The third scam to watch out for is online shopping scams. These scams involve cybercriminals posting fake ads for products that seem too good to be true. When you click on the ad, you are taken to a website that looks legitimate but is a scam. So, be sure to do your research before buying anything online, and only buy from websites that you trust.

By being aware of these scams and taking steps to protect yourself, you can have a safe and enjoyable Amazon Prime Day!

Apartment Rental Scam:

Are a common type of cybercrime. In these scams, the attacker tricks the victim into paying for a rental apartment that does not exist. The attacker may spoof an email from a legitimate rental company or use a fake website to collect payment. Victims may also be tricked into giving away personal information, such as their social security number or bank account information.

To protect yourself from apartment rental scams, verify any rental company's legitimacy before sending any payments. Do not give away your personal information unless you are sure you are dealing with a legitimate company. Always be aware of red flags, such as spelling mistakes or incorrect contact information on websites or emails.

Business Email Compromise Scam:

It is a cyber-attack that uses email to access confidential information. BEC attacks are hazardous because they often spoof the email address of a high-ranking executive within the company. This makes it difficult for employees to differentiate between legitimate and illegitimate emails. As a result, businesses can fall victim to BEC attacks even if they have implemented strong cyber security measures.

There can be severe consequences if a business falls victim to a BEC attack. For example, the company may lose money due to fraudulent transactions conducted by the attacker. The business may also experience damage to its reputation as a result of the attack.

Businesses should use two-factor authentication and strong passwords to protect themselves from BEC attacks. They should also be wary of emails that contain suspicious attachments or links. In addition, companies should regularly audit their networks for vulnerabilities that cyber attackers could exploit.

Auto Warranty Scam:

Are rising, with crooks pocketing more than $1 billion in fraudulent claims yearly. According to the National Insurance Crime Bureau (NICB), bogus warranty schemes have become the third most common type of insurance fraud.

One of the most common scams is using a "phantom car." A phantom car is a vehicle that doesn't exist but is listed on an auto warranty contract. The scammer will submit a claim for damages to the nonexistent vehicle and collect the payout.

Another common scam is the "casualty scam." In this scam, the scammer will damage a car by crashing it into something and then file a claim for damages. When filing a claim, they often use a fake name, driver's license, and insurance policy number.

Caregiver Fraud Scam:

One of the most common cyber security threats is caregiver fraud. In caregiver fraud, cyber criminals pose as caregivers to gain access to their victim's personal information. The cybercriminals may then use this information to commit identity theft or other scams.

There are several steps that you can take to protect yourself from caregiver fraud, including:

- being aware of the signs of caregiver fraud
- checking the credentials of any caregiver that you hire
- using strong passwords and security measures
- monitoring your bank and credit card statements for suspicious activity

Celebrity Impostor Scam:

Cybersecurity is essential in today's digital age. Unfortunately, cybercriminals always look for new ways to exploit vulnerabilities to steal data or money. One of the latest scams that cybercriminals use is the "Celebrity Impostor Scam."

In this scam, cybercriminals pose as a celebrity on social media or in an email and try to convince people to send them money or personal information. They might promise prizes or rewards in exchange for this information. Sometimes, they even create fake websites or social media profiles to make themselves look more credible.

If you're ever contacted by someone claiming to be a celebrity, and they ask for money or personal information, be very careful. It's important to remember that stars would never ask for this type of information online. If you're not sure whether the offer is legitimate, it's best to err on the side of caution and not respond.

Census Scam:

Cyber security scams are rising, and the Census is no exception. Be on the lookout for fake Census surveys that attempt to steal your personal information. Remember, the Census will never ask for your social security or credit card number. If you receive a suspicious survey, do not respond and report it to the FTC.

Charity Scam:

Cyber security is a critical issue for all individuals and businesses. Unfortunately, cybercriminals always look for new ways to exploit people and organizations. One of the latest scams is charity scams.

A charity scam is a scam in which a cybercriminal tries to convince people to donate money to a fake charity. The cybercriminal may create a fake website or social media profile for the charity. They may also use emails, phone calls, or text messages to get people to donate money.

Charity scams can be very convincing. Cybercriminals may use pictures of sick children or animals or claim that the money will be used to help victims of a natural disaster. They may even create fake websites that look very similar to legitimate charities.

If you are thinking about donating money to a charity, be sure to do your research first. Make certain the charity is legitimate and that it has a good reputation. You can also check the website of the Better Business Bureau to see if there are any complaints about the charity.

If you think a charity has scammed you, report it to the Federal Trade Commission (FTC).

Coronavirus Scam:

Cyber security scams are rising as people become more desperate for information about the virus. Be on the lookout for phishing emails, fake websites, and other scams that try to steal your personal information. Protect yourself by visiting trusted websites and not clicking on links or downloading attachments from unknown sources. Identity theft is also a risk during a pandemic, so keep your personal information safe and secure.

If you're on Medicare, beware of scammers promising free COVID-19 tests.

These scammers are calling people and running websites and ads, trying to get people to give them their Medicare information. Once they have your information, they'll bill Medicare for fraudulent charges.

We're hearing reports of many Medicare recipients who signed up for these free COVID-19 tests and never received them. What's worse is that the scammers could also bill for other products and services that people didn't need - and didn't get.

If you're on Medicare, be sure to avoid any offers for free COVID-19 tests. If you're contacted by someone offering these tests, hang up or delete the email. And if you think you may have been scammed, report it to Medicare immediately.

- Don't give out your personal information, like your Medicare number, to anyone you don't know and trust.

- Don't believe any offers that seem too good to be true, like free COVID tests.

- Report any suspicious activity to the FTC.

Credit Card Interest Rate Scam:

Cyber security is more important than ever, as online scams and identity theft are rising. One of the most common scams is the credit card interest rate scam. In this scam, the attacker sends an email or text message to the victim, asking them to update their credit card information. The letter includes a link to a website where the victim can enter their credit card information. However, the website is fake, and the credit card information has been stolen.

To protect yourself from this scam, never enter your credit card information into a website that you are not sure is legitimate. Always ensure that the website has a secure connection (indicated by a green lock in the address bar) and that the URL starts with "HTTPS." Also, check for spelling and grammatical errors in any messages from unfamiliar senders, as these are often signs of a scam.

Credit Repair Scam:

Credit repair scams are a type of cyber security scam in which scammers attempt to steal personal information or money from people to fix their credit. These scams can take many forms, such as phishing emails, phone calls, or text messages.

Credit repair scams often promise to fix credit problems for a fee, but they usually do not deliver on their promises. Credit repair scams can also damage your credit score if they successfully steal your personal information.

If you think you may have been the victim of a credit repair scam, there are several steps you can take to protect yourself. First, report the fraud to the Federal Trade Commission (FTC). You can also contact your state Attorney General's office or the Better Business Bureau.

You should also monitor your credit report and score regularly to ensure no new fraudulent accounts have been opened in your name. You can get a free copy of your annual credit report from www.annualcreditreport.com. You can also get a free credit score from www.creditkarma.com.

Cruise Scam:

Cruise scams are designed to trick you into giving away your personal information or money, so it's essential to be vigilant against them.

Some common tips for avoiding cruise scams include being aware of what you're signing up for, never giving out your personal information online, and being careful about where you're clicking. If something seems too good to be true, it probably is. Do your research before booking any trips and trust only reputable sources.

Cryptocurrency Fraud Scam:

It is a type of cybercrime that involves stealing or fraudulent activities involving cryptocurrencies. Cryptocurrency fraud can include scams such as phishing attacks, cyber-attacks, and Ponzi schemes. Victims of cryptocurrency fraud can lose money or cryptocurrency.

Cryptocurrency fraud is a growing problem, and cybercriminals are increasingly targeting cryptocurrency users. Victims of cryptocurrency fraud should report the crime to the police and file a complaint with the Federal Trade Commission.

1. Make sure to research any cryptocurrency investment before moving. Be sure to investigate who is behind the currency and their motives.

2. Always use a reputable and secure wallet provider when investing in cryptocurrencies.

3. Beware of fake or phishing websites that may try to steal your personal information or steal your cryptocurrencies.

4. Keep your computer software up-to-date, and be sure to have a good antivirus program installed.

Debt Collection Scam:

One of the most common cyber security threats is the debt collection scam. In this scam, the attacker sends an email or text message to the victim pretending to be from a collection agency. The message asks the victim to pay their debt immediately, or they will be sued. The victim may also be asked to provide their personal information, such as their Social Security number or bank account information.

1. Don't ignore the calls. If a debt collector is harassing you, don't avoid their calls. Respond clearly and concisely and ask them to stop contacting you at work or home.

2. Get everything in writing. If the debt collector asks for payment, get all agreements in writing. This will help protect you from any false claims or future scams.

3. Check your credit report regularly. Keep an eye on your credit report for any unauthorized activity. This can help you catch any scammers before they do too much damage.

4. Report any suspicious activity. If you think a debt collector is scamming you, report it to the FTC immediately. This will help protect other consumers from being targeted by the same scammer."

Debt Relief Scam:

Are a type of cybercrime that targets individuals struggling to pay off their debts. The scammers promise to help the victims reduce or eliminate their debts, but instead, they steal the victims' money. Debt relief scams can occur through phone calls, emails, or social media messages.

To protect yourself from debt relief scams, always be wary of unsolicited offers and never give out your personal information or money to someone you don't know. Also, be sure to check the legitimacy of any debt relief company before working with them. You can check the company's Better Business Bureau (BBB) rating and reviews.

Dietary Supplement Scam:

Many Americans are duped by dietary supplement scams every year. These scams promise miraculous results, such as weight loss, muscle gain, improved health, and more. However, most of these supplements are ineffective, and some can even be dangerous.

The best way to avoid dietary supplement scams is to do your research. Look for credible sources of information and be skeptical of any claims that seem too good to be true. Always consult with a doctor before starting any new supplement regime.

Disaster Scam:

Are a common type of cyber scam. These scams often involve emails or phone calls that claim to be from a legitimate organization such as a bank, insurance company, or government agency. The scammer asks the victim to provide personal information or make a payment.

One common disaster scam is the "emergency evacuation" scam. This scam involves an email or phone call that claims to be from a government agency or other organization. The scammer tells the victim that there is an emergency and that they must evacuate their home or office. The scammer then asks the victim for personal information such as their Social Security number or bank account information.

Another common disaster scam is the "disaster relief" scam. This scam involves an email or phone call that claims to be from a charity or other organization. The scammer typically asks the victim for money to help with disaster relief efforts.

Be careful of emails or phone calls that claim to be from a legitimate organization and ask for personal information or money. If you are unsure whether an email or phone call is legitimate, contact the organization directly to ask for confirmation. Do not provide personal information or make any payments until you know the communication is honest.

DMV Scam:

Cyber security is essential for preventing scams like those at Department Motor Vehicle (DMV) offices. In these scams, cybercriminals pose as DMV employees to get personal information like Social Security numbers and driver's license numbers. This information can then be used to commit identity theft.

To protect yourself from these scams, always be suspicious of unsolicited emails and phone calls from people who claim to be from the DMV. Never give out your personal information unless you are sure the person is legitimate. Also, keep your computer's firewall and antivirus software up to date.

Email extortion Scam:

They are a type of cyber-attack in which the attacker sends an email to the victim threatening to release sensitive data or harm the victim if a ransom is not paid. The email may include a link to a website where the victim can make the payment. Email extortion scams are often successful because the victim may fear having their personal information released or being harmed.

To protect yourself from email extortion scams, never open attachments or click links in emails from unfamiliar senders. Additionally, keep your antivirus software up-to-date and use strong passwords.

Fake Check Scam:

One of the most common cyber security threats is the fake check scam. In this scam, an attacker sends a victim a check for more than the amount owed and asks the victim to wire the difference back. The victim wires the money, but the bill eventually bounces, and the victim is out of the money they wired.

To protect yourself from fake check scams, be cautious when accepting checks from people you don't know. Verify that the check is legitimate and that the funds are available in the account before wiring any money. If you are unsure whether a check is legitimate, contact your bank.

Free Trial Scam:

Cyber security scams are a problem that companies face daily. Attackers use various methods to try and steal sensitive data or money from businesses. One common cyber security scam is the free trial scam. Attackers send emails to businesses offering free security software trials in this scam. The email usually looks like it came from a legitimate company, such as Microsoft or Symantec.

The free trial scam aims to get businesses to download and install the software on their computer. Once the software is installed, the attacker can access the business's data or take control of the computer. To avoid falling victim to a free trial scam, companies should be careful when clicking on email links and always check the sender's legitimacy.

Funeral Scam:

Although cyber security is critical to protecting your online presence, it's not the only threat you face. Scammers are always looking for new ways to steal your money or identity, and one of their favorite tactics is the funeral scam.

In a funeral scam, scammers pose as funeral home directors or employees. They contact the family of a recently deceased person and offer to handle the funeral arrangements. The scammers ask for a deposit to cover the cost of the funeral, but they never hold the funeral or return the money.

Be careful when selecting a funeral home to protect yourself from funeral scams. Check with the Better Business Bureau to see if there are any complaints against them. Never give out personal information or pay a deposit without seeing proof of services. And if you suspect that you're being scammed, report it to the police.

Gas Pump Skimming Scam:

If you've ever had your credit card information stolen, it was via a gas pump skimmer. Gas-station fraud is all too common, and skimmers are small devices that thieves place on or above the card readers at gas pumps (and ATMs) to copy and steal your credit card information.

Gas pump skimmers can do a real number on your bank account. Gas-station fraud commonly occurs with skimmers, small devices that thieves place on or above the card readers at gas pumps (and ATMs) to copy and steal your credit card information.

Additionally, always pay attention to your credit card transactions. Check your account statement regularly and report any unauthorized charges immediately.

There are several ways to detect a skimmer, but one of the easiest is to check the card reader itself. Often, skimmers will not have an authentic card reader and will instead be a separate piece that is attached to the machine. If something looks off about the card reader or is loose, it's best to avoid using it. You can also try to wiggle the card reader part of the machine; if it moves, then there is a good chance it is not legitimate.

Gift Card Scam:

Gift cards are for gifts, not for payments. As soon as someone tells you to pay them with a gift card, that's a scam. Gift cards are popular with scammers because they're easy for people to find and buy. They also have fewer protections for buyers compared to some other payment options.

One way to avoid gift card scams is to only buy gift cards from reputable, well-known merchants. Another way to avoid gift card scams is to use gift cards that have been activated and have the funds available. You can also avoid gift card scams by not sharing the gift card number and PIN with anyone.

Impostor Scam:

They are a type of cyber-attack that tricks users into giving away personal information or money. The scammer typically poses as a trusted individual or organization, such as a bank, government agency, or tech company. The scammer may ask for personal information such as your Social Security number or bank account details. They may also ask for money to fix a computer problem or to unlock your device.

If you receive a phone call, email, or text message from someone asking for personal information or money, be suspicious. Do not give out any information or send money. Contact the organization that the scammer claims to represent to verify their identity. You can also report the scam to the Federal Trade Commission (FTC).

Investment Scam:

Cyber security is vital for everyone, especially regarding investment fraud. Scammers often try to exploit people by stealing their money or personal information. Be sure to stay safe online and watch out for any suspicious activity. Identity theft is also a common scam, so protect your personal information. Do your research before investing in any stocks or other financial products. Stay safe online and be aware of the dangers that cyber criminals pose.

1. Do your research
2. Stay safe online
3. Beware of fake emails and websites
4. Be skeptical of too-good-to-be-true offers
5. Keep your financial information confidential
6. Contact authorities if you think you've been scammed
7. Stay informed about investment scams

IRS Impostor Scam:

It is a type of cybercrime in which criminals pose as IRS agents to steal money or personal information from victims. The scam begins with a phone call in which the victim is told that they owe money to the IRS and must pay immediately. The caller may also ask for personal information such as Social Security or bank account numbers. If the victim refuses to pay or provides incorrect information, the caller may threaten legal action or arrest.

The IRS Impostor Scam is a sophisticated scam that can be difficult to detect. However, several signs can indicate that you are being scammed, including:

- Demanding payment immediately
- Asking for personal information
- Threatening legal action or arrest

If you believe you are the victim of an IRS Impostor Scam, contact the IRS immediately and report the incident. Do not provide any personal information to the caller, and do not make any payments.

Jury Duty Scam:

Cybersecurity is critical for everyone, especially those required to perform jury duty. Jury duty scams are a common way for cybercriminals to try and steal your personal information. In these scams, you may receive a phone call or email from someone pretending to be from the court system, asking you to provide personal data like your Social Security number or driver's license number. Be very careful about giving personal information in response to communication you didn't initiate.

If you're ever unsure about the legitimacy of communication-related to jury duty, contact the court system in your area directly to ask about it. Never respond to unsolicited requests for personal information and keep your computer and mobile devices protected with antivirus software and strong passwords.

Medical Equipment Scam:

A type of cybercrime is when criminals attempt to steal money or information by posing as legitimate medical equipment suppliers. They may use fake websites or emails to trick victims into paying for products they never receive. Medical equipment scams can be costly and can result in the loss of sensitive personal information.

To protect yourself from medical equipment scams, always verify the legitimacy of a supplier before making a purchase. Never provide your credit card information or other personal details to a supplier you do not trust. Be especially careful when purchasing medical equipment online, as many fake websites may attempt to steal your money.

1. Always ask for referrals from friends and family before purchasing medical equipment.

2. Research the company online before making a purchase. Look for reviews and complaints.

3. Make sure the company has a physical address and phone number. If they do not, avoid doing business with them.

4. Ask the company for proof of insurance and licensing.

5. Get a written warranty and return policy before making a purchase.

Medical Identity Theft Scam:

It is a type of cybercrime that involves stealing someone's personal information to gain access to their medical records. Attackers can use this information to fraudulently bill insurance companies or to get medical treatment using someone else's name. Medical identity theft can also be used to obtain prescription drugs or sell someone's medical information for profit.

There are several steps you can take to protect yourself from medical identity theft, including:

- Keeping your personal information confidential
- Monitoring your credit report and credit score
- Protecting your computer with antivirus software
- Avoiding phishing scams

Medicare Card Scam:

Are a type of cybercrime in which criminals attempt to steal the personal information of Medicare beneficiaries. The thieves use this information to bill Medicare for medical services that were never provided fraudulently.

The best way to protect yourself from Medicare card scams is to protect your personal information. Do not give out your Social Security or Medicare number unless you have to. Be careful online, and only use secure websites when submitting sensitive information.

If you believe you have been the victim of a Medicare card scam, report it to the Centers for Medicare and Medicaid Services (CMS) immediately. You can report it online or by phone.

Medicare Fraud Scam:

Are a type of cybercrime that involves stealing money from the Medicare program. The perpetrators of Medicare Fraud often use stolen identities to submit false claims for reimbursement. Medicare Fraud can be very costly for the government and cause financial harm to patients and healthcare providers.

There are several steps that you can take to protect yourself from Medicare Fraud scams:

- -Be suspicious of anyone who offers to help you submit a Medicare claim for reimbursement.

- -Do not give out your personal information, such as your Social Security number, to anyone who contacts you unsolicited.

- -Check if the company or individual is registered with the Centers for Medicare and Medicaid Services (CMS).
- -Report any suspicious activity to the CMS Fraud Hotline.

Money Mule Scam:

Are a common type of cybercrime. In a money mule scam, an attacker tricks someone into transferring money to them. The funds may be transmitted through wire transfers, online payments, or cryptocurrency. Money mules are often recruited through online advertisements or social media posts.

To avoid becoming a victim of a money mule scam, be wary of any online advertisements or social media posts that offer too-good-to-be-true opportunities. Be sure to do your research before agreeing to any financial transactions. Contact your local law enforcement agency if you suspect you may have been involved in a money mule scam.

Mortgage Relief Scam:

An attacker's attempt to steal sensitive data or money from individuals or organizations is a cyber security scam. The attackers may pose as representatives of legitimate companies or organizations, or they may create fake websites or emails to lure victims into giving up their personal information.

Mortgage relief scams can be very costly for victims and can also result in the loss of important personal information. It is essential to be aware of the signs of a mortgage relief scam and to take steps to protect yourself from these attacks.

Some tips to protect yourself from mortgage relief scams include:

- Never provide your personal information or credit card number to someone you do not know or trust.

- Always verify the legitimacy of a company or organization before providing them with any personal information.

- Be cautious about unsolicited emails and websites, and never click on links or download attachments from unknown sources.

- If you think a mortgage relief scam may have targeted you, report it to the police and your credit card company immediately.

Moving Scam:

They can be very costly for businesses, so taking steps to protect yourself is vital. Cybersecurity solutions such as Zero Trust Pro-Active Cyber Security can help you stay safe online and protect your data from attackers.

Cyber security is a critical issue for all businesses, and moving scams are one of the most common threats. A moving scam is when an attacker poses as a legitimate moving company to steal money or personal information from their victims.

There are several steps businesses can take to protect themselves from moving scams, including verifying the legitimacy of the moving company and using encryption for sensitive data.

To check the legitimacy of a moving company, you can do a quick online search for reviews or visit the Better Business Bureau website. You can also call the company to ask for references from past customers.

Nigerian Scam:

These are cyber scams in which attackers attempt to trick victims into sending money. The attackers typically pose as someone who needs help transferring money out of Nigeria or a company representative looking to hire employees. The scammers may also pose as friends or family members of the victims and ask for money to be sent to them.

Victims who fall for Nigerian scams can lose a lot of money. Sometimes, the scammers may even convince victims to travel to Nigeria to collect money. Victims should be cautious when responding to any offers that seem too good to be true. Be suspicious of unsolicited emails or phone calls asking for personal information or money.

- -Don't give out your personal information or bank account number to anyone you don't know.

- -Never send money to someone you don't know.

- -Report any suspicious activity to the police.

Obituary Scam:

They are cyber-attacks that use obituaries to trick people into revealing personal information. The scammer sends an email or text message pretending to be from a funeral home and asks for the deceased person's date of birth, Social Security number, and other personal information. The scammer can use this information to steal the victim's identity or to access their bank account.

Tips for avoiding obituary scams:

- Do not respond to emails or text messages asking for personal information about the deceased.

- Check the funeral home website mentioned in the email or text message. The email or text message is likely a scam if it is not listed on the funeral home's website.

- Contact the funeral home directly if you have questions about an email or text message.

Online Banking Scam:

Cyber security is more critical now than ever before. As you may have heard, there have been many online banking scams lately in which cybercriminals attempt to steal your personal information or money. One of the best ways to protect yourself from these scams is to be aware of the different types of scams that are out there.

Some of the most common online banking scams include the following:

Phishing Scam:

In these scams, cybercriminals send you emails or text messages that appear to be from your bank or another trusted organization. These scams aim to get you to click on a link or download a file containing malware. Once the malware is installed, it can steal your personal information or money.

Vishing scams:

Are similar to phishing scams, but cybercriminals use phone calls to get your personal information instead of emails or text messages. They may call you and say they are from your bank or another trusted organization and ask for your account number, password, or other personal information.

Malware Scam:

In these scams, cybercriminals install malware on your computer to steal your personal information or money. The malware can be installed when you click an email link or download a file. It can also be installed when you visit a website infected with malware.

Smishing Scam:

These are similar to phishing but use text messages instead of emails. The goal of smishing scams is to get you to click on a link or download a file that contains malware.

If you want to protect yourself from online banking scams, here are some tips:

- Be aware of the different types of scams that are out there.

- Never click on links or download files from emails or text messages unless you are sure they are from a trusted source.

- Never give out your personal information unless you are sure the person asking for it is legitimate.

- Install antivirus software and keep it up to date.

- Keep your computer's operating system and software up to date.

- Create strong passwords and never use the same password for more than one account.

Pharmacy Scam:

They are a common type of cyber scam. These scams occur when criminals create fake online pharmacies to steal people's personal information or money.

To avoid pharmacy scams, only purchase medications from reputable pharmacies. Be sure also to check the website's security features, such as a secure HTTPS connection and a valid SSL certificate. Never enter your personal information into an unsecured website.

If you think you may have been scammed, report the incident to the Federal Trade Commission (FTC).

Online Shopping Scam:

When you're shopping online, be careful of fake or fraudulent websites. Some common scams include:

- Phishing scams: A scammer sends an email or text message that appears to be from a legitimate company, such as your bank or credit card company. The letter asks you to click on a link or provide your personal information. The link takes you to a fraudulent website that looks like the real thing.

- Bogus websites: A scammer creates a phony website that looks like a legitimate site, such as an online store. The scammer tries to trick you into entering your personal information, such as your credit card number or login credentials.

- Fake pop-ups: You may see a pop-up on your computer screen that appears to be from a legitimate website, such as your bank or credit card company. The pop-up asks you to provide personal information or download software. If you enter your information or download the software, you may give the scammer access to your computer and confidential information.

To protect yourself from online shopping scams, follow these tips:

- Always check the web address before entering any personal information. The web address should start with "HTTPS" and include a lock symbol. This means that the website is secure and your information is encrypted.

- Never provide your personal information unless you're sure the website is legitimate. Don't enter your credit card number, login credentials, or other sensitive information unless you're sure the site is safe.

- Be skeptical of emails or text messages that ask for personal information. Don't click on any links in these messages; don't provide personal information unless you're sure the sender is legitimate.

- Don't download software from unknown sources. If you're unsure whether a program is safe, don't download it.

- Use strong passwords for all of your online accounts. A strong password is hard to guess and includes numbers, letters, and special characters.

Package Scam:

They are a common way for cyber criminals to steal personal information or money from unsuspecting victims. Here are a few tips to help you avoid becoming a victim:

- Never give out your personal information, such as your address, credit card number, or Social Security number, unless you know the person or company you're dealing with is reputable.

- Be suspicious of unsolicited emails or phone calls asking for personal information. Don't click on any links or download any attachments in these emails, and don't give out any personal information over the phone unless you're sure the person who called is legitimate.

- Review your credit report regularly to catch any unauthorized activity. You can get a free copy of your credit report every 12 months from each of the three major credit reporting agencies at AnnualCreditReport.com.

Pet Scam:

The best way to avoid pet scams is to be vigilant and skeptical of online ads. If an offer seems too good to be true, it probably is. Be especially cautious of ads requiring you to pay for a pet before receiving it.

If you are interested in purchasing a pet, do your research first. Check out reputable pet adoption websites or local animal shelters to find a pet that is right for you. And always be sure to meet the pet in person before handing over any money.

Phishing Scam:

Phishing is a scam where cybercriminals try to trick you into revealing your personal information. They do this by sending you fake emails or texts that appear to be from legitimate companies or organizations. The goal of phishing is to steal your identity or financial information.

Here are some tips on how to avoid phishing scams:

- -Never click on links or download attachments from emails you don't recognize.

- -Be suspicious of emails that ask for personal information, such as your address, Social Security number, or bank account details.

- -Look for the lock icon in the browser bar to ensure the website is encrypted.

- -Verify the legitimacy of a website by checking its address and contact information.

- -Use strong passwords and two-factor authentication whenever possible.

If you think you may have been scammed, report it to the Federal Trade Commission (FTC) at ftc.gov/complaint.

Phone Scam:

1. Don't answer calls from unknown phone numbers.

   Don't answer the phone if you don't know who is calling. Scammers often use random or unknown phone numbers to try and scam people. If you answer the phone and the caller starts asking for personal information, hang up immediately.

2. Be aware of common scams.

There are many typical scams that scammers use to try and steal your personal information. Some cons include fake calls from the IRS, emails asking for money, and calls from tech support promising to fix your computer. Be aware of these scams and know how to protect yourself from them.

3. Use strong passwords and two-factor authentication.

    One way to protect yourself from cybercrime is to use strong passwords and two-factor authentication. This means using a password that is difficult to guess and combining it with a second form of authentication, such as a security token or a one-time code sent to your phone. This will help to keep your account secure even if your password is compromised.

Political Scam:

They can be particularly damaging because they often target the emotions of passionate people about a particular issue. Here are a few tips for protecting yourself from political scams:

-   Be skeptical of emails or calls that claim to be from a political organization or candidate.

-   Do research before giving any money or personal information to a political organization or candidate.

- Look for legitimate contact information (website, phone number, email address) on the official website of the organization or candidate.

- Don't open attachments or click on links in emails from unknown sources.

Ponzi and Pyramid Scam:

They are scams that promise high investment returns but instead use money from new investors to pay off earlier investors. To protect yourself from these schemes, it's essential to be aware of the warning signs:

- Promises of high returns with little or no risk

- Unclear or exaggerated advertising claims

- Requests for personal information such as social security or bank account numbers

- Pressure to make a decision quickly

- Unsolicited emails or calls from someone you don't know

If you think you may have been scammed, report it to the Federal Trade Commission (FTC) at FTC.gov/complaint.

Psychic Scam:

There are a few simple ways to protect yourself from psychic scams:

- Never give out your personal information, such as your address, social security number, or credit card number.

- Be skeptical of any claims that seem too good to be true. Legitimate psychics will not make outlandish promises.

- Request references from the psychic and check them thoroughly.

- Get a second opinion from another psychic if you're unsure about something.

- Never send money to a psychic in exchange for services.

Public Wi-Fi Scam:

Public Wi-Fi is a convenient way to stay connected when you're out and about, but it can also be a haven for cybercriminals looking to steal your personal information. Here are a few tips for protecting yourself from public Wi-Fi scams:

- Use a VPN: A virtual private network (VPN) creates an encrypted tunnel between your device and the VPN server, protecting your data from prying eyes.

- Use strong passwords: Make sure your passwords are strong and unique and don't use the same password for multiple accounts.

- Be aware of phishing scams: Phishing scams are emails or websites that attempt to lure you into revealing your personal information. Be wary of unsolicited emails or links, and never enter your personal information unless you're sure the website is legitimate.

- Keep your software up to date: Make sure you install all updates for your software and operating system, as these updates often include security patches that can help protect your device from cyber threats.

- Install anti-virus software: Anti-virus software can help protect your device from malware and other cyber threats. Make sure you keep your anti-virus software up to date and run regular scans to help keep your device safe.

QR Code Scam:

Are a type of cyber scam that can target consumers and small businesses. These scams involve malicious QR codes that redirect users to fake or fraudulent websites. To protect yourself from QR code scams, only scan codes from trusted sources, and always check the website address before entering personal information.

Ransomware Scam:

Ransomware scams are becoming more common and sophisticated, so it's important to be aware of the risks and take steps to protect yourself. Here are a few tips:

- Make sure your computer is protected with anti-virus software and a firewall.

- Be careful what you click on - don't open emails or attachments from unknown sources.

- Keep your software up to date.

- Back up your data regularly.

- If you do fall victim to a ransomware scam, disconnect your computer from the internet immediately.

Reverse Mortgage Scam:

As a consumer or small business, it's essential to be aware of the different types of scams that are out there. One scam that is becoming more common is the reverse mortgage scam. This scam typically targets seniors and can result in the victim losing their home and savings.

There are a few things you can do to protect yourself from reverse mortgage scams:

- -Be aware of any offers that seem too good to be true. If it sounds too good to be true, it probably is!

- -Do your research. Make sure you know whom you're dealing with, and check with trusted sources to ensure the company is legitimate.

- -Talk to someone you trust about any offers that come your way. It's always best to get a second opinion before making any decisions.

If you think you may have been targeted by a reverse mortgage scam, please contact your local authorities.

Robocall Scam:

There are many ways to protect yourself from robocalls, and some are more effective than others. One of the most important things you can do is to register your phone number with the National Do Not Call Registry. This will help to reduce the number of calls you receive from telemarketers. You can also install call blocker software on your phone, which will help to screen calls and block known scammers. Another option is to use a landline phone instead of a cell phone, as landlines are less likely to be targeted by scammers. Finally, carefully review any calls or messages that seem suspicious, and do not give out any personal information without verifying the caller's identity.

Romance Scam:

If you're looking for love online, be careful of romance scams. These scams involve someone you've been chatting with online asking for money, often claiming to be in trouble. To protect yourself from romance scams, here are a few tips:

- Don't send money to someone you've just met online. This is a red flag that someone might be trying to scam you.

- Don't share your personal information with someone you don't know well. This can include your address, phone number, or email address.

- Don't respond to any requests for money, no matter how convincing the story might be.

If you think you might be a victim of a romance scam, report it to the authorities.

Secret Shopper Scam:

The Federal Trade Commission (FTC) has some great tips on how to protect yourself from Secret Shopper Scams:

- Be suspicious of unsolicited emails or phone calls that promise a high income for minimal work, especially if the offer requires you to wire money or sign up for a program before receiving your first payment.

- Do your research. Check the FTC's website or consumer protection agency in your country to see if there are any warnings about the company or program.

- Don't give out your personal information, such as your bank account number, unless you know and trust the company.

- If it sounds too good to be true, it probably is.

Shopping Scam:

Scammers target back-to-school shoppers in a variety of ways. They may create fake websites that sell counterfeit or inferior products. They may also send phishing emails, pretending to be from a well-known retailer, to steal your personal information. Be sure to check the refund and return policies of any website before you make a purchase, and never give out your personal information or credit card number through email.

When shopping online, be sure to:

Look for the lock symbol in your browser's address bar and make sure the web page starts with "HTTPS" (instead of just "HTTP"). This indicates that the site has a secure connection and that your information is being encrypted.

Only enter your credit card information on secure websites. Look for the padlock symbol in your browser and make sure the web page address starts with HTTPS.

Be wary of emails that ask you to click on a link to update your account information or take advantage of a special shopping offer. These may be phishing scams designed to steal your personal information.

Check the seller's reputation online before making a purchase. Read reviews from other customers and compare prices on different websites before making a purchase.

SIM Card Scam:

As more and more people rely on their cell phones for everyday communication, scammers are increasingly targeting victims with sim card scams.

- Always keep your sim card information confidential
- Never give out your sim card number or password to anyone

- If you think you may have been a victim of a sim
  card scam, contact your service provider
  immediately.

One way to protect yourself against sim card scams is to
password protect your sim card. This will make it more
difficult for the perpetrator to access your information. You
can also monitor your account activity regularly and report
any suspicious activity to your cell phone carrier.

Small Business Scam:

There are a few key things you can do to protect yourself
from small business scams:

- -Be aware of the red flags. Watch out for emails or
  calls that seem too good to be true or ask for
  personal information like your Social Security
  number.

- -Never give out your personal information without
  verifying the source's legitimacy.

- -Secure your devices and networks with strong
  passwords and anti-virus software.

- -Educate yourself about common scams and how to
  avoid them.

If you suspect you may have been scammed, report it to the
FTC at ftc.gov/complaint.

Smishing Scam:

Smishing is a type of cyber scam where you receive a text message that appears to be from a legitimate source, such as your bank or credit card company. The message will ask you to click on a link or call a phone number to take care of an issue with your account. However, if you do this, you will give the scammers access to your personal information.

To protect yourself from Smishing scams, never click on links or call phone numbers in unsolicited text messages. Instead, open your web browser and go directly to the website of the company that sent the message. If you have any concerns about an account issue, call the company directly using the number on their website or your billing statement.

Social Media Scam:

Social media scams are becoming increasingly common and target consumers and small businesses. Here are some tips for protecting yourself:

- Be wary of unsolicited messages or links, especially if they appear to be from a friend or trusted source.

- Do not click on any links or open any attachments unless you are sure they are safe.

- Use strong passwords and change them regularly.

- Install anti-virus software and keep it up to date.

- Be cautious about what information you share online.

- Review your privacy settings and make sure you are only sharing information with people you trust.

- Report any suspicious activity to the police or your internet service provider.

Social Security Scam:

There are a few key things you can do to protect yourself from social security scams:

- Be vigilant. Be suspicious of unsolicited calls, emails, or texts from people asking for your personal information. Never give your social security number or other sensitive information to someone you don't know and trust.

- Know the warning signs. Watch out for fake websites, emails, or phone calls that appear to be from the Social Security Administration (SSA). The SSA will never ask for your social security number or other personal information via email or phone.

- Stay informed. Keep up to date on the latest scam trends and how to protect yourself. The SSA provides helpful information on its website about common scams and how to avoid them.

Spear-Phishing Scam:

One of the most common cyber security threats faced by consumers and small businesses is spear-phishing. This is when cybercriminals send fraudulent emails that appear to be from a trusted source, such as a bank or credit card company. The goal of spear-phishing is to trick the recipient into clicking on a link or opening an attachment, installing malware on their computer.

There are several steps you can take to protect yourself from spear-phishing attacks:

- Never open attachments or click on links in emails from unknown sources.

- Verify the legitimacy of any email you receive by contacting the company directly. Do not reply to the email, as this could give the cybercriminal access to your account.

- Use a strong password and change it regularly.

- Install up-to-date antivirus software and keep it updated.

- Enable two-factor authentication wherever possible.

Student Loan Scam:

One of the most common types of scams targeting consumers is student loan scams. These scams can take many forms, such as phishing emails or phone calls from fake loan servicers. They often promise to help students get a lower interest rate or consolidate their loans, but in reality, they just want to steal your personal information or money.

To protect yourself from student loan scams, never share your personal information or bank account details with anyone you don't trust. Also, research before choosing a loan servicer and only work with reputable companies. You can also check the Better Business Bureau (BBB) website to see if a company has any complaints filed against it.

Survey Scam:

One common scam that can target consumers and small businesses is survey scams. These scams typically involve someone posing as a market researcher or survey taker and asking for personal information such as your name, address, or Social Security number. They may also ask you to participate in a survey, promising a prize.

To protect yourself from survey scams, never give out any personal information unless you are sure of the source's legitimacy. Also, be wary of any surveys that require you to pay money upfront, as these are likely scams. Finally, never click on links in unsolicited emails or text messages from people you don't know; these may contain malware that could infect your device.

Sweepstakes and Lottery Scam:

Lottery and sweepstakes scams are common and can be very costly. Here are a few tips to help protect yourself:

- Never give out personal information, such as your social security number or bank account information, to someone you don't know.

- Don't respond to emails or calls asking for money upfront to claim a prize.

- Be skeptical of any offers that seem too good to be true.

- Always check with the Better Business Bureau or another reliable source to ensure a company is legitimate before giving them your personal information.

- Never send money or give credit card information to someone you don't know.

If you think you may have been scammed, report it to the FTC at ftc.gov/complaint.

Tax ID Theft Scam:

One of the most common cyber security threats faced by consumers and small businesses is tax ID theft. This occurs when someone obtains your personal information, such as your Social Security number, to file a fraudulent tax return in your name. There are several things you can do to protect yourself from this type of scam:

- Guard your personal information carefully. Do not share your Social Security number or other sensitive information unless you trust them.

- File your taxes as early as possible. This will minimize the time someone has to steal your identity and file a fraudulent tax return in your name.

- Use a secure Wi-Fi network when filing your taxes online. Make sure the website you are using is encrypted and has a valid security certificate.

- Check your credit report regularly for signs of fraud. If you notice anything suspicious, contact the credit bureau immediately.

In addition, be sure to monitor your credit report regularly for any signs of fraud. If you suspect you have been the victim of tax ID theft, contact the IRS immediately. They will help you file a report and work to resolve the issue.

Tax Preparation Scam:

Tax preparation scams are rising, and cybercriminals are getting more sophisticated in their methods. Here are a few tips to help protect yourself from tax preparation scams:

1. Be aware of common scams. There are many tax preparation scams, so be aware of the most common ones. Some of the most common scams include phishing emails, fake calls from the IRS, and malware attacks.

2. Use caution when opening emails. Be especially cautious when opening emails that appear to be from the IRS or other tax-related organizations.

These emails often contain malicious attachments or links that can infect your computer or steal your personal information.

3. Stay up to date with the latest security threats. Keep your antivirus software up to date and install any security updates released for your operating system. This will help protect you from malware and other cyber threats.

4. Use strong passwords. Make sure to use strong passwords for your online accounts, and don't use the same password for multiple accounts. This will help reduce the chances of your accounts being compromised if your password is stolen by cybercriminals.

5. Be careful about giving out your personal information. Don't give out your personal information unless you're sure that you can trust the person or organization asking for it. Cybercriminals can use this information to steal your identity or commit fraud.

Tech Support Scam:

Cyber security threats can be sophisticated and targeted at consumers and small businesses. One of the most common cyber security threats is the Tech Support Scam. This scam occurs when a cybercriminal posing as a tech support representative calls a victim and tries to trick them into giving away personal information or installing malware on their computer.

To protect yourself from this scam, it's important to be aware of the warning signs. Some common warning signs include:

- The caller asks for your personal information, such as your name, address, or credit card number

- The caller tries to rush you into making a decision or installing software

- The caller tells you that your computer is infected and offers to help you fix it

If you receive a call like this, you must hang up and report it to the authorities. You can also install cyber security software on your computer to help protect yourself from malware and other cyber threats.

Time-Share Resale Scam:

Time-share resale scams are on the rise, with victims losing an estimated $36 million in 2017. So how can you protect yourself from this type of scam?

Here are a few tips:

1. Don't trust unsolicited phone calls or emails from unfamiliar companies offering time-share resales.

2. Do your research! Check the company's website and reviews online to see if they are legitimate.

3. NEVER send money upfront to purchase a time-share. Legitimate companies will not require payment until you have received the time-share.

4. Get everything in writing. Make sure any contracts or agreements are in writing and include contact information for the company in case you have questions or need to dispute charges.

5. If it sounds too good to be true, it probably is. Be skeptical of any offer that seems too good to be true – it likely is a scam.

Travel Scam:

When traveling, it's essential to be aware of the many different types of travel scams that can occur. Here are some tips for avoiding them:

- Do your research before booking any travel arrangements. Be sure to read reviews and compare prices.

- Avoid dealing with unauthorized or unknown agents. Only deal with reputable companies.

- Make sure you have a copy of your travel arrangements, including flight numbers and hotel reservations, and keep these in a safe place.

- Beware of any offers that seem too good to be true. If something seems too good to be true, it probably is.

- Never give out your personal information such as your credit card details or passport number unless you're sure of the legitimacy of the company you're dealing with.

- If you suspect a scam, report it to the police or to the relevant authority in the country you're visiting.

Following these tips will help protect you from travel scams and ensure a safe and enjoyable holiday experience.

Update Account Scam:

cyber security scams are becoming more sophisticated and prevalent, so it's important to be aware of the risks and take steps to protect yourself.

One common scam is the 'Update Account' scam, where cybercriminals try to trick you into providing your personal information or login credentials. They may do this by sending you an email or message that looks like it's from a legitimate company or organization, such as your bank, credit card company, or social media site. The email or message may ask you to update your account information or provide additional details.

However, the email or message is actually from cyber criminals, and they will use your personal information to steal your money or identity. So be very careful about any emails or messages that ask you to provide personal information, and never click on any links or attachments in those emails.

If you think you may have been targeted by a cybersecurity scam, contact your bank, credit card company, or social media site immediately. And remember to always keep your computer software up-to-date and use strong passwords to protect your accounts.

Utility Scam:

Utility scams are common scams that can target consumers and small businesses. These scams involve someone pretending to be from a utility company, such as a phone or electricity provider, and trying to trick you into paying for bogus services or products.

To protect yourself from utility scams, it's important to be aware of the signs of a scam and know how to protect your personal information. Here are some tips:

- Be suspicious of unsolicited calls or emails from utility companies, especially if they ask for payment or personal information.

- Never give out your personal information or credit card number over the phone or online unless you are sure you are dealing with a legitimate company.

- Always check your utility bill carefully for suspicious charges and report any discrepancies to the utility company immediately.

- Keep your computer protected with antivirus software and a firewall and update your software regularly.

-   If you think you may have been scammed, report it
    to the police and the Federal Trade Commission.

Vacation Scam:

When traveling, it's important to be aware of vacation scams. These scams can target anyone but often prey on people unfamiliar with the area they are visiting. Common scams include offers for fake cheap airfare or accommodation, unauthorized taxi drivers, and tickets to tourist attractions that are not legitimate.

To protect yourself from vacation scams, always do your research before booking any travel. Check reputable sources like travel websites or the government tourism office website for information on attractions and deals in the area you're visiting. If something sounds too good to be true, it probably is - don't fall for cheap airfare or accommodation scams.

Be wary of unsolicited offers from strangers, especially if they seem too good to be true. Don't share your personal information with anyone you don't know and trust. If you're ever in doubt about an offer, contact your local police department for advice.

By being aware of the risks and taking precautions, you can help protect yourself from vacation scams.

VA Pension Poaching Scam:

If you're a veteran or the surviving spouse of a veteran, you may be eligible for a VA pension. However, some scammers target veterans and their families to steal their pensions. Here are some ways to protect yourself from VA pension poaching:

- -Be aware of any offers that seem too good to be true. Poachers may promise veterans high payouts or exaggerated benefits, but these offers are almost always scams.

- -Do your research. Many reputable organizations can help you apply for a VA pension, so be sure to do your research before working with any organization you don't know.

- -Check the legitimacy of the organization. Organizations that solicit veterans for their pensions should be registered with the VA, so be sure to check the legitimacy of any organization before giving them your personal information.

- -Stay vigilant. If you think you may have been targeted by a pension poaching scam, report it to the VA immediately.

Veterans Charity Scam:

How to protect yourself from Veterans Charity Scam:

- Be aware of common scams and how they work.

- Don't respond to unsolicited emails, phone calls, or text messages.

- Don't give away personal information, such as your Social Security number or credit card number.

- Verify the legitimacy of any charity before donating. You can do this by checking the charity's website or contacting the Better Business Bureau.

Veterans Scam:

There are a few things you can do to protect yourself from Veterans Scams. First, be aware of the red flags: unsolicited calls or emails, high-pressure tactics, requests for personal information, and offers that seem too good to be true. Secondly, be skeptical of any organization that asks for money upfront, especially if it claims to be a veteran's charity. Finally, do your research! Verify the legitimacy of any organization before donating or providing personal information.

Weight-Loss Scam:

There are a few things you can do to protect yourself from weight-loss scams:

- -Be skeptical of ads that promise quick and easy weight loss. These schemes are bogus and will likely not help you lose weight.

- -Do your research before signing up for a weight loss program. Read reviews online and talk to people who have tried the program.

- -If you're considering weight loss surgery, consult with a qualified doctor first. Many risks are associated with such surgeries, and they should only be performed by a qualified physician.

- -Be aware of common red flags of scam weight loss programs, such as high-pressure sales tactics, unrealistic claims, and charges for products or services that should be free.

- By being proactive and aware of the risks, you can protect yourself from falling victim to a scam weight loss program.

Who's Who Scam:

One of the most common scams targeting consumers and small businesses is the Who's Who scam. In this scam, a con artist will pose as a representative of a well-known company or organization and try to get you to reveal personal information or send money.

There are a few things you can do to protect yourself from this scam:

- -Never give out your personal information or credit card number to someone you don't know.

- -Be suspicious of any unsolicited phone calls, emails, or letters asking for personal information.

- -Check with the company or organization mentioned in the call, email, or letter to see if they contacted you.

- -Never send money to someone you don't know.

If you think you may have been targeted by a Who's Who scam, report it to the Federal Trade Commission (FTC) at ftc.gov/complaint.

Work-From-Home Scam:

There are a few things you can do to protect yourself from work-from-home scams:

- Do your research. Be sure to research any company you're considering working for, and check for reviews online.

- Be wary of offers that seem too good to be true. If the work sounds too easy or the pay is much higher than average, it's likely a scam.

- Ask for proof of employment. Legitimate employers will be happy to provide you with proof of employment, such as an ID badge or paystubs.

- Avoid giving out personal information. Don't share your Social Security number, bank account information, or other sensitive information unless you're 100% sure the company is legitimate.

By following these tips, you can help protect yourself from work-from-home scams and other cyber security threats.

Child Tax Credit Scam:

If you're a parent, you may be targeted by scammers who claim they can help you get a more considerable child tax credit. They might even say they can get the money for you upfront before filing your taxes.

Please don't fall for it! There's no way to increase your child tax credit without first filing your taxes. And if someone claims they can get you the money upfront, they're probably just trying to steal your personal information or your money.

If you're ever contacted by someone claiming to be able to help you with your child tax credit, hang up the phone or delete the email right away. Please don't give them any of your personal information.

Cloud Access Job Scam:

If you're looking for a job in the cloud computing industry, beware of scammers trying to take advantage of people.

There have been reports of scammers posting fake job ads on websites and social media platforms, promising high-paying jobs with well-known companies. But when people apply for the jobs, they're asked to pay a fee for "training" or "certification."

In some cases, the scammers may even ask for personal information, such as a Social Security number or bank account number, which could be used to steal your identity.

If you come across a job ad that seems too good to be true, do your research to ensure it's legitimate. And never pay any fees to apply for a job.

Emergency Broadband Program Impersonator Scam:

If you're experiencing financial hardship and are seeking assistance with your internet service, be aware that scammers may try to take advantage of you. The Federal Communications Commission (FCC) is warning consumers of a new scam involving people posing as representatives of the Emergency Broadband Benefit Program (EBBP).

These scammers contact people by phone, email, text message, or social media and falsely claim to be associated with the EBBP. They may ask for personal information such as your name, address, date of birth, Social Security number, bank account information, or credit card number to sign you up for the program or access your benefits.

Don't fall for this scam! The FCC will never contact you asking for your personal information. If you receive a suspicious call, email, text message, or social media post, please report it to the FCC's Consumer Center.

Google Voice verification Scam:

The Google Voice verification scam is a phishing scheme that tricks people into giving away their personal information. The scammer will pose as a Google representative and ask for your name, address, and credit card number to verify your account. They may even promise to give you a free month of service if you provide this information. However, once they have your information, they will use it to make unauthorized charges on your credit card or steal your identity. This scam can be very costly and dangerous, so it's essential to be aware of it and avoid falling victim to it.

If you receive a suspicious email or call asking for your personal information, do not respond. Hang up the phone or delete the email immediately. You should also report the incident to Google so that they can investigate it.

Omicron PCR testing Scam:

PCR (polymerase chain reaction) is a common laboratory technique used in molecular biology to amplify a segment of DNA. It is used to make copies of DNA strands, making them easier to study. Forensic science also uses PCR to identify genetic markers in samples taken from crime scenes.

Many companies offer PCR testing services. However, many scam artists are looking to take advantage of people familiar with this technology. It is essential to do your research before choosing a company to perform your PCR testing.

One way to protect yourself from being scammed is to ask the company for references from past customers. You can also check online reviews to understand what other people have said about the company's services. Another thing to look for is whether the company is accredited by an organization like the American Association for Laboratory Accreditation (A2LA).

When it comes to PCR testing, it is always better to be safe than sorry. Do your homework and choose a reputable company before proceeding with any tests.

Post Disaster Scams:

Natural disasters like hurricanes, floods, and earthquakes cause billions of dollars yearly. And unfortunately, scammers see these events as opportunities to take advantage of people who are already struggling.

There are a few different types of post-disaster scams that you should be on the lookout for:

1. Fake charities: After a major disaster, it's common for scammers to set up fake charities purporting to help victims. They may contact you by phone, email, or even in person. Be sure to research before donating to any charity, and never give out personal information like your Social Security number or credit card number.

2. Price gouging: Businesses dramatically increase prices for essential goods and services like food, water, shelter, and gasoline. If you see costs for these items skyrocketing, report it to your local authorities.

3. Home repairs: Many people may need repairs after a natural disaster but don't have the money to pay for them. Be careful if you're approached by someone offering home repair services, as there may be scammers trying to take advantage of you. Get references and do your research before hiring anyone to work on your home.

4. Insurance scams: After a disaster, it's common for scammers to try to scam people out of their insurance money. They may offer to help file a claim or promise to get you a bigger payout. Be sure to consult with an insurance

professional if you need help filing a claim, and never give out personal information or money to someone you don't know.

5. Repair scams: Many people may be trying to take advantage of homeowners who need repairs after a natural disaster. Be careful if someone approaches you offering home repair services, and always get multiple estimates before choosing a contractor. Never pay upfront for any repairs, and be sure to check references carefully.

Prop Money Scams:

Several scams use prop money as bait. These scams often involve someone trying to sell counterfeit money or fake merchandise. The scammer will often try to get the victim to purchase the prop money or fake merchandise with real money. In some cases, the scammer will even try to get the victim to invest in a business venture that doesn't exist.

Prop money scams can be difficult to spot because the prop money can look very realistic. If you're ever offered the opportunity to buy prop money or fake merchandise, be sure to do your research before handing over any cash. And if you're ever asked to invest in a business venture, make sure you know everything about the company before you write a check.

Zelle payment scam:

Zelle is a digital payment platform that allows users to send and receive money. It is a safe and convenient way to transfer money, but some risks are associated with using the service.

One of the biggest dangers of using Zelle is the potential for scams.

There have been reports of scammers using the service to defraud people. In one common scam, a user will receive a text message or email from someone claiming to be from Zelle. The message will say that the recipient has been sent a payment from someone they know. They will then be directed to click on a link to claim the money.

Once the link is clicked, it will take the user to a website that looks like the official Zelle website. The site will request the user's personal information, such as their name and bank account number. The site may also ask users to verify their identity by providing a selfie. Once the information is entered, the scammer will have access to the user's bank account and can withdraw money from it.

To avoid being scammed, it is vital to be aware of the warning signs. Be wary of any unsolicited messages asking for personal or financial information. Do not click on any links in the news, and do not enter any confidential information on the website. If you are unsure whether a message is legitimate, contact your bank or Zelle directly.

Credit Freeze

Immediate Action Steps to Take

If you're concerned about becoming a victim of cybercrime or identity theft, one of the best things you can do is to place a security freeze on your credit file. This will prevent prospective creditors from accessing your credit report, making it much harder for them to open new accounts in your name.

A security freeze is also sometimes called a credit freeze. Either way, it's an important tool for protecting yourself from fraud and identity theft. And it's something everyone should consider, especially if they've been the victim of a data breach or cyberattack.

To place a security freeze on your credit file, you'll need to contact each of the three major credit bureaus: Equifax, Experian, and TransUnion. The process is simple, but there are a few things you'll need to know first.

The fee for placing a security freeze on your credit file is generally $5-$10 per bureau, although it may be waived in some cases. And you'll need to provide some personal information, including your name, Social Security number, and date of birth.

Once you've placed the freeze with each bureau, it will remain in effect until you lift it or remove it altogether. So, if you're planning on applying for credit shortly, you'll need to remember to lift the freeze before you do.

It usually takes just a few minutes to place a security freeze on your credit file. But keep in mind that it may take a little longer if you need to contact each of the three credit bureaus separately.

I have included the online links to freeze your credit:

- https://www.transunion.com/credit-freeze

- https://www.equifax.com/personal/credit-report-services/credit-freeze/

- https://www.experian.com/freeze/center.html

Do Not Call Registry

The national do not call registry lists phone numbers that telemarketers are not allowed to call. If you sign up for the registry, your number will be added, and telemarketers should stop calling you. However, there are some exceptions to this rule.

For example, charities and political organizations may still call you even if you're on the registry. This is because they're not covered by the rules of the registry. Additionally, scam artists may still try to call you even if your number is on the registry. That's why it's crucial to protect yourself from scam phone calls using cyber security measures like anti-virus software and spam filters.

If you're on the national do not call registry, you may still get calls from telemarketers. In some cases, these calls may be from scammers trying to steal your personal information. Here's what you need to know about the do not call registry and how to protect yourself from scam phone calls.

The national do not call registry is a list of phone numbers that telemarketers are not allowed to call. If you sign up for the registry, your number will be added, and telemarketers should stop calling you. However, there are some exceptions to this rule.

For example, charities and political organizations are allowed to call people on the registry, as long as they are not selling anything. And, if you have given your number to a company and agreed to be called by them, they can still call you.

How do I add my number to the DO NOT Call Registry?

To add your number to the national do not call registry, visit donotcall.gov. You can also call 1-888-382-1222 from the U.S. to register your number.

To sign up for the do not call registry, you can register your home or mobile phone for free.: https://www.donotcall.gov/

How long will it take for sales calls to stop?

It can take a while for sales calls to stop after you sign up for the registry. Some telemarketers may not be aware of the registry, so they may continue to call you. You can report any unwanted calls to the Federal Trade Commission (FTC).

Will my registration Expire?

No, your registration on the national donot call registry will not expire. However, you may need to renew your registration if you move or change your phone number.

Can I add my cell phone number to the Do Not Call Registry?

Yes, you can add your cell phone number to the registry. You can also register your landline and fax numbers. However, keep in mind that registering your number does not guarantee that you will not receive calls from telemarketers. Some telemarketers may still call you even if your number is on the registry.

Will the Registry stop all unwanted calls?

No, the registry will not stop all unwanted calls. There are some exceptions to the do not call registry, such as political organizations and charities. Additionally, telemarketers may still call you if you're on the list but have recently made a purchase from their company.

Can a company still call me with a sales pitch?

Yes, companies can still call you with a sales pitch, even if you're on the national do not call registry. However, there are some exceptions to this rule. For example, charities and political organizations may still call you.

Are any other types of calls still allowed under FTC rules if I'm on the Registry?

There are some exceptions to the do not call registry. You may still receive calls from telemarketers if they are trying to sell you something that is not covered by the registry, like insurance or investments. Additionally, you may still get calls from companies whom you have an existing business relationship with or if you have given them permission to call you.

What about Robocalls?

Robocalls are automated phone calls that sometimes play a recording and connect you to a live person. They often offer free products or services, but they're scams. You can't always tell if a call is a robocall just by looking at the number. Sometimes scammers spoof caller ID to make it look like the call is coming from a legitimate company or organization. The best way to protect yourself from robocalls is to use caller ID blocking features on your phone and never give out your personal information in response to an unsolicited phone call.

If phone scammers violate the Do Not Call list rules, they may be subject to civil and criminal penalties.

This could include a fine of up to $16,000 per call. They could also be sent to prison for up to five years. It's important to follow the registry rules and protect yourself from scam phone calls.

Multi-Factor Authentication (MFA)

Is a security system that requires more than one form of authentication to verify the user's identity. This can include something the user knows (like a password), something the user has (like a phone or keycard), or something the user is (like a fingerprint). MFA can be used to protect all your computers and online accounts, including email, banking, and social media.

To set up MFA on your computer, you must download and install an MFA program like Duo or Google Authenticator. Once the program is installed, you must create an account and add your devices (such as your phone or laptop). Once your devices are added, you can log in to your accounts using MFA.

To set up MFA on your online accounts, you must log in and find the security or authentication settings. In most cases, you will be able to find MFA under two-factor authentication or two-step verification. Once you have enabled MFA, you can log in to your account using your username and password, plus a verification code from your device.

Remove Personal Information from Data Brokers

Most people are unaware that their private information is readily available online. Search sites like Spokeo and Pipl expose sensitive personal information such as your name, age, home address, phone number, email addresses, family members, other people associated with you, your income range, credit score range, political preferences, criminal records, and much more.

There is no one-size-fits-all answer to this question, as the best way to remove your private information from data broker websites will vary depending on the specific website. However, some tips on how to remove your private information from data broker websites include:

- Searching for your name and contact information on the website, and then contacting the website directly to ask them to remove your information.

- Filling out a form on the website that allows you to request that your information be removed.

- Contact the webmaster of the website and ask them to remove your personal information.

If you are having difficulty removing your private information from a data broker website, or if you would like assistance in doing so, you can contact an online privacy protection service for help.

You can also hire a 3rd party company to do all the heavy lifting. OneRep is a leading provider of online privacy protection services. They can help you delete your private information from people-search sites, protecting you from identity theft, stalking, and other crimes.

Contact OneRep today to learn more about how they can help you delete your private information "from people-search sites, and protect you and your family from identity theft, stalking, and other crimes." Visit https://onerep.com/

There are many different types of malware, but some of the most common ones include: - Viruses: These are self-replicating programs that can damage or disable your computer. - Trojans: These are malicious programs that masquerade as legitimate software. They can allow hackers access to your computer system. - Worms: These are programs that replicate themselves and spread through computer networks. They can cause extensive damage to systems and networks. - Spyware: This type of malware collects information about you without your knowledge. It can then send this information to cybercriminals.

What is spyware?

Spyware is a type of malware that can be installed on a computer without the user's knowledge, typically to collect information about the user or their activities. Spyware can also be used to track keystrokes, steal passwords, or log-in credentials, and even take screenshots of the user's activity. Some spyware may also be designed to install other types of malware on the user's computer.

What is adware?

Adware is a type of malware that displays advertisements on an infected device. Adware can be very disruptive and intrusive and can even slow down a device's performance.

What is a bot?

A bot is a type of malware that is often used to send spam or conduct other malicious activities.

What is ransomware?

Ransomware is a type of malware that cybercriminals use to hold computer files for ransom. The cybercriminal will encrypt the files on the computer and demand payment to release the files. Ransomware can be very costly and can cause a lot of damage to the victim's computer.

What is scareware?

Scareware is a type of malware that tricks users into paying for unnecessary security software. It typically pops up on the screen as a warning, telling the user that their computer is in danger and that they need to purchase the software to fix the issue.

What is a rootkit?

A rootkit is a type of malware that gives cybercriminals access to your computer. It allows them to steal your identity and sensitive information, as well as control your computer.

What is a virus?

A virus is a type of malware that, when executed, replicates by infecting other computer files or programs.

What is a trojan horse?

Trojan horses are a type of malware that disguises itself as a legitimate program. Once installed, it can allow cyber criminals access to your computer or networks. Trojan horses can also be used to steal your personal information or financial data.

What is a worm?

A worm is a type of malware that self-replicates and spreads to other computers. Worms can consume a lot of resources on a computer, slowing it down or even causing it to crash. They can also be used to steal information or passwords.

What is a man in the middle?

A man-in-the-middle attack is when a cybercriminal intercepts communications between two parties, usually to steal personal information or financial data. The attacker inserts themselves into the communication process, either by tampering with the data or by pretending to be one of the parties involved. This can allow the cybercriminal to gain access to sensitive information that would otherwise be protected.

What are the symptoms of malware?

Symptoms of malware can include anything from strange pop-ups on your computer to complete system crashes. In some cases, you may even lose access to your files or have them stolen by malware. If you think you may be infected, it's best to take your computer to a professional for help.

Cybercriminals are always looking for ways to exploit unsuspecting victims and steal their personal information or valuable belongings. By being aware of the different types of malware out there and taking steps to protect your data and privacy, you can make it much more difficult for these criminals to succeed.

There are a few key things you can do to protect your devices and personal data from cybercriminals: - Use strong passwords that are difficult to guess. - Install security software and keep it up-to-date. - Avoid opening suspicious emails or clicking on links in them.- Be careful when using public wireless networks. Make sure to use a secure connection if possible. - Back up your data regularly in case it is compromised or lost.

How to use public Wi-Fi safely

If you're using public Wi-Fi access, it's important to be aware of the risks involved. Public Wi-Fi is unsecured, which means that anyone on the same network as you can see what you're doing online. This makes it a prime target for cybercriminals who want to steal your personal information or infect your device with malware.

To protect yourself while using public Wi-Fi, make sure you use a VPN. A VPN encrypts all your traffic and keeps it private, so no one can see what you're doing online. It also protects you from hackers who may be trying to steal your data.

If more than one hotspot appears claiming to belong to an establishment that you're in, check with the staff to avoid connecting to an imposter hotspot. cybercriminals often set up fake Wi-Fi networks to steal your information. So, make sure you only connect to legitimate hotspots and be careful about what information you share while connected.

When you're browsing the internet, it's important to make sure that all of the websites you exchange information with have "HTTPS" at the beginning of their web address. This ensures that your transmitted data will be encrypted, and therefore, much less likely to be stolen by cybercriminals.

One way to help keep your information safe from cyber criminals is to install an app add-on that forces your web browsers to use encryption when connecting to websites. This will help to protect your information, even when you are visiting well-known sites that may not normally encrypt their communications.

You can adjust your smartphone's settings so that it does not automatically connect to nearby Wi-Fi networks. This gives you more control over where and when you connect. By being more vigilant about which networks you connect to, you can help protect yourself from cyber criminals who might want to steal your information.

When transmitting sensitive information, using your cellphone data plan instead of Wi-Fi may be more secure. This is because Wi-Fi signals can be intercepted by cybercriminals, while cellphone data plans are typically more secure.

Bluetooth Security

If you have anything of value, the criminals want it. That's why it's so important to keep your Bluetooth security settings always turned on. If you're not using Bluetooth, turn it off. This will help protect your information and prevent cybercriminals from gaining access to your device.

Home network wireless security:

If you have anything of value, the cybercriminals want it. They can steal your identity and access your personal information, so it's important to protect your home wireless network with security measures. Here are a few tips to help keep your network safe:

1. Use a strong password that is not easily guessed.

2. Change your password often.

3. Make sure your router is password protected.

4. Install antivirus and malware protection software on all of your devices.

5. Be aware of what you are downloading and opening online.

6. Only connect to trusted networks."

Safeguard your wireless router:

As cyber criminals become increasingly sophisticated in their attacks, it is more important than ever to protect your data with encryption. Wireless routers often come out of the box with the encryption feature disabled, so be sure it is enabled soon after the router is installed. This will help ensure that your data is safe from prying eyes.

If you have a wireless network in your home, it's important to protect it by changing the network's default SSID. This is the name that appears when someone searches for wireless networks nearby. cybercriminals often use default SSIDs to try and gain access to your network. By changing the SSID, you make it more difficult for these criminals to find your network and attempt to steal your data.

As cyber criminals become more sophisticated, they are increasingly targeting wireless routers. This is because cybercriminals often target wireless routers and try to guess the default password. By gaining access to the router, they can not only steal your personal information but also control your Internet access.

There are several steps you can take to protect your router and your personal information. First, change the default password on your router. Second, make sure your firewall is turned on. Third, update your firmware regularly. Fourth, use strong passwords and encryption methods. Finally, keep your software up to date.

If you follow these steps, you can help protect yourself from cybercrime and keep your personal information safe.

If you have anything of value, the criminals want it. This means that your personal information, financial data, and other sensitive information is at risk of being stolen by cybercriminals. One way to help protect yourself from cybercrime is to use a MAC address filter in your wireless router. This will help to ensure that only devices that you trust can connect to your wireless network.

By turning off your router when you're not using it, you can make it more difficult for them to gain access to your data.

Data backup

The best way to protect yourself is to back up your data regularly. This will ensure that if your data is ever compromised, you will have a copy to restore.

So, what can you do to make sure your files are gone? According to cyber security experts, the best way to delete a file permanently is to use a secure-erase tool. This will overwrite the file with random data multiple times, making it impossible to recover.

Social media sharing

One of the best ways to protect yourself from cyber criminals is to not share too much on social media. Criminals can use this information to piece together enough information to steal your identity or hack into your accounts. So be careful about what you post online and make sure your privacy settings are enabled.

E-mail and web browser privacy:

One of the best ways to protect yourself from cyber criminals is to be vigilant about your privacy when using email and the web. Here are some tips to help you stay safe:

- Use a strong password for your email account, and don't use the same password for multiple accounts.

- Be careful about what information you share online. Don't post personal information like your address

or phone number and be cautious about sharing too
much information in emails and on websites.

- Use a reputable antivirus program and keep it up to
date.

- Install a firewall on your computer.

- Be careful when clicking links in emails and on
websites. Make sure the website is reputable before
entering any personal information.

- If you're using a public computer, don't save your
passwords or login information.

Ultimately, it is your responsibility to safeguard your data,
your identity, and your computing devices When you send an
email, should you include your medical records? Probably not
– unless you are comfortable with the idea that
cybercriminals could gain access to them. The same holds for
any other type of information that you might store on your
computer or mobile device. Cybercriminals are becoming
increasingly sophisticated in their attacks, so it is important
to take steps to protect yourself from identity theft and other
types of cybercrime. One way to do this is by using a Web
browser that provides privacy protection features such as
Private Browsing mode or Incognito mode.

These modes help to keep your browsing history and other
personal information private from prying eyes. Another thing
you can do is install security software on all of your devices
and keep it up-to-date. Security software helps to protect
against malware and other types of cyber threats. Finally, be

careful about what kind of information you share online and with whom you share it. Remember that cybercriminals are very good at social engineering – they will try to trick you into giving away sensitive information like passwords or credit card numbers. By taking some simple precautions – like using privacy protection features in your Web browser.

How to Blur Your House in Google Maps Street View

To blur your house in Google Maps' Streetview, you'll need to first find your house on the map. You can do this by searching for your address or zooming in on your neighborhood. Once you've found your house, click on the "Streetview" icon in the bottom right-hand corner of the screen.

Once you're looking at an image of your house, look for the teeny-tiny "Report a Problem" link in the lower-right corner. This will open up a window where you can provide feedback about the image. Under the "Privacy" tab, you'll be able to blur your house by clicking on the "Blur my house" button.

After clicking on the "Blur my house" button, you'll be taken to a screen that allows you to fine-tune the appearance of the image. Make sure the targeting box covers your entire house.

1. Click on the "My home" button.
2. Enter your email address into the text field.
3. Click on the "Submit" button.

After submitting your request, you should receive a status update in your email inbox. If Google needs more information from you, it will reach out to you directly. Otherwise, the blurring process should take place relatively quickly.